Spiritual Manipulation: I Survived the Man That I Prayed For

A Memoir of Faith, Deception, and Deliverance

by Angela L. Jackson

A powerful testimony of spiritual awakening, emotional survival, and the rebirth of a woman who reclaimed her identity.

Copyright Page

Copyright © 2026 Angela L. Jackson

All rights reserved.

No part of this book may be reproduced, distributed, or transmitted in any form or by any means — electronic, mechanical, photocopying, recording, or otherwise — without the prior written permission of the author, except in the case of brief quotations used in reviews or scholarly works.

This book is a work of memoir based on the author's personal experiences and reflections. Names, identifying details, and certain circumstances have been changed to protect privacy. Any resemblance to actual persons, living or dead, or actual events is coincidental. This narrative reflects the author's perceptions and emotional truth and is not intended to diagnose, accuse, or define the character of any individual.

ISBN: 9798278745297

Printed in the United States of America

First Edition

Dedication

Dedicated to **Sarah**, who inspired me, saw my vision, and gently affirmed that this book needed to be written. Thank you for believing in the work before it had a name. As it is written in our favorite film, *The Color Purple*, "Nothing but death can keep us from it."

To my dear friend, **Ms. Cynthia**,

Thank you for being there — for your silent prayers, your presence, and your patience. You walked this journey with me and witnessed everything that lives within these pages. Thank you for the late-night phone calls, the mentorship, the counsel, and the spiritual guidance you so selflessly gave.

And to **my mother**, thank you for standing beside me during one of the darkest seasons of my life. Thank you for your prayers, your strength, and your unwavering love. Thank you for being the perfect mother to me.

I didn't lose my faith.

I lost my silence.

And in that breaking,

I found myself again.

-Angela L. Jackson

Author's Note

Posture Shift was born from poetry — from the language of healing that rises when two broken hearts encounter love and something within them begins to change. It was written in the space where tenderness still existed, where hope had not yet been fully questioned, and where faith was holding everything together.

This book continues that journey.

What you are reading is a memoir drawn from my personal experiences and reflections during a season that requires a deeper kind of honesty. It is written from my perspective and shaped by what I understood, believed, and felt at the time these events unfolded. While *Posture Shift* captures the shift toward love and connection, these pages explore what followed — the discernment, the unraveling, and the quiet awakening that came after.

To protect the privacy of those involved, names, identifying details, and certain circumstances have been changed. This story is not intended to diagnose, accuse, or define the character of another person. Instead, it examines the emotional and spiritual impact of a relationship in which devotion and control became entangled, leaving confusion where clarity was meant to live.

What I experienced did not happen suddenly. Spiritual confusion rarely announces itself. It often arrives gently, wrapped in prayer, compassion, and good intentions. Understanding came gradually, through distance, reflection, and grace, as I learned to listen again to my own inner knowing.

My intention is not to tell readers what to believe or how to heal. This book, like *Posture Shift*, offers language rather than instruction. If you recognize yourself in these pages, know that questioning what once felt sacred is not betrayal, and choosing clarity does not mean you have abandoned love or faith.

I invite you to read slowly and with care. Pause when needed. Honor what rises. Healing is not linear, discernment takes time, and transformation often begins not with answers — but with the courage to tell the truth.

TABLE OF CONTENTS

Prologue
The First Shift 9

Chapter One
The Girl Who Was Healing 12

Chapter Two
The Night the Music Lied 23

Chapter Three
The Fault Line Beneath the Fantasy 32

Chapter Four
When God Pulled Back the Curtain 55

Chapter Five
Why Leaving Was Not Simple 84

Chapter Six
The Night the Windows Shattered 88

Chapter Seven
When *What If* Becomes a Trap 96

Chapter Eight
The Shift That Saved Me 101

Chapter Nine

The Day the Spell Broke **112**

Chapter Ten

The Tactics: How Spiritual Manipulation Shows Up

.... **121**

Chapter Eleven

The Rising — When God Restores What Was Stolen

.... **127**

Epilogue

Posture Shift: *I Survived the Man That I Prayed For*

.... **133**

A Blessing for the Reader **138**

Dear Heavenly Father **139**

PROLOGUE — The First Shift

I didn't recognize the moment when my heart first tilted out of alignment.

It didn't happen with a loud crack or a dramatic collapse. It happened quietly — the way a picture frame slips crooked on the wall after a door closes too hard.

First you don't notice the shift. Then one day you see it, and you wonder how long it's been that way. My life, my love, my faith — all of it had been sitting slightly tilted.

I kept trying to straighten myself up using the same hands that had broken me.

And each time, I whispered to God, "Fix me," without realizing He'd already given me the courage to fix myself.

There comes a moment — a holy moment — when a woman realizes that the battle she's been fighting is not against the man who betrayed her, but against the version of herself that believed she had to accept it.

My moment came in a whisper.

Not a scream.

Not a storm. A whisper that slid down into the place where my fear lived and said,

"You don't have to live like this anymore. "That whisper was the beginning of my shift.

A shift in how I saw love.

A shift in how I prayed.

A shift in how I stood up inside my own spirit.

A shift in how I walked toward healing, even when my legs trembled.

This book is not about the man who broke me. It's about the woman who rose after being broken.

It's about the quiet courage buried inside a tired heart.

The kind of courage that doesn't roar hums. It steadies itself.

It waits patiently for the moment you're ready to hear it.

It's about the girl I used to be, the one who loved with her whole chest, even when she should've protected herself.

And it's about the woman I became, the one who learned that love is not proven by how much pain you can endure.

This is my posture shift.

The moment my spirit stopped leaning toward people who couldn't hold me,

and instead leaned back into the God who always had.

If you're holding this book, maybe you've felt that shift too that quiet suspicion that your heart has been tilting for too long, and that somewhere inside you, a new beginning is asking to be born.

If so, come with me. Let's stand up straight again —in truth, in healing, in tenderness,

and in the kind of love that doesn't break us to keep us. This is where my story begins.

Not in the heartbreak, but in the moment, I decided I deserved more than surviving.

Welcome to the shift.

CHAPTER ONE: The Girl Who Was Healing

Opening Lesson: *Healing begins the moment you stop apologizing for your own pain.*

Before I ever met him, I was already stitching myself back together. I was a church girl—raised in the pews, shaped by Scripture, and grounded in faith. My father was an ordained minister; my grandmother served faithfully as the church nurse, and my grandfather was a deacon in the Baptist church.

Sundays were never optional. There was Sunday School in the morning, Vacation Bible School in the summer, drill team practice, morning service, and night service. Church wasn't an event; it was a lifestyle. Learning and studying the Bible came naturally.

On my mother's side, the story wasn't very different. They were deeply rooted in the Pentecostal church before branching out into Baptist and non-denominational ministries. My foundation was built on prayer, worship, and the belief that God was always near.

In my twenties, I escaped a relationship that had bruised both my skin and my spirit. I promised myself I would never lose my voice like that again. I packed my things, moved to a quieter part of town, and rebuilt a sanctuary for myself—one small choice at a time.

I enrolled in community college. I was a young adult now, making grown-woman decisions, but my love for Christ hadn't changed. I found a church that felt like home. I surrounded myself with peace. I prayed, fasted, and attended service faithfully. Slowly, I began to breathe again. I found a space where healing didn't feel like work, it felt like returning to myself.

I was becoming a woman again, not just a survivor, not a shadow, not a broken vessel, but a woman with goals, dreams, and dignity.

My home was quiet. My routine was steady. My soul was finally learning to unclench.

I wasn't looking for love.

Love was the last thing on my mind.

But healing has a way of making you shine again.

And sometimes, broken people mistake your light for an invitation.

I met Kai Turner on a day that felt completely ordinary. I had picked up my friend Keisha Monroe for our morning shift, and she had already brought him up once before.

"Angela, I'm going to introduce you to someone," Keisha said. "You two would be perfect for each other."

I laughed and shook my head. "No thank you. I'm focused on me right now."

But that morning, when he climbed into the back seat of my car, something unexpected happened.

I was playing an old gospel hymn—*Trouble Don't Last Always* by Rev. Timothy Wright—a song that had carried me through heartbreak, loneliness, and nights when my tears soaked the pillow. That song had seen me at my lowest.

I expected silence from him, maybe a little small talk.

Instead, from the backseat came a familiar sound...

He was singing.

Not humming.

Not mumbling.

But singing every single word with the kind of passion that only rises from a heart that needs that song as much as I did.

I was shocked.

His tough exterior didn't match his voice at all. His tone carried conviction—raw, earnest, almost pleading. It intrigued me. For a moment, I knew there was more to him than what met the eye. And in that moment, I learned a lesson I should've held onto longer:

Maybe you shouldn't judge a book by its cover.

When we arrived at work, he stepped out of the car, turned back toward me with quiet confidence, and said:

"My name is Malachi Turner... but my friends and family call me Kai."

The way he said it—soft, intentional—made something in me pause. Names carry stories, and his felt like an introduction to a chapter I didn't know I was about to live.

At that time, I was on a spiritual walk, hungry for anything that felt like God. Hearing him sing *Trouble Don't Last Always*, word for word, with pain and hope woven together, made me wonder if our spirits were traveling in the same direction.

But healing can play tricks on you.

It can make you believe recognition is destiny.

It can make you hear compatibility where there's only coincidence.

So I didn't think much of it that day.

We worked in the same building but on different sides, so it was easy to let curiosity fade.

Until one afternoon.

I stepped outside frustrated—mentally drained from the toxic environment of that workplace. Kai said something friendly to me, and I brushed him off without hesitation. At that stage in my Healing had left me with no room, no patience, and no desire for a new man—
especially not one who appeared out of nowhere.

But God has a way of letting people cross your path more than once when there's a lesson attached.

My coworker Keisha—the same one who insisted Kai and I were meant to meet—didn't come to work one day. But Kai did. He needed a ride, and I just happened to be the one driving.

I won't pretend a small part of me wasn't excited.
It felt like an opportunity to ask him questions, to learn who he really was beneath that quiet confidence.

Somewhere between casual conversation and the rhythm of the road, he told me he was a minister.

We talked lightly on the way in.
His voice carried that soft confidence of a man who had lived a life he wasn't afraid to share.

And when our workday ended, we ended up in my car again.

I needed to stop by the grocery store before taking him home. Out of respect, I asked if he minded.

He said, "Sure, I don't mind."

And he came in with me. Lord, is this the man that I prayed for?

Somewhere between the produce aisle and the frozen section, pieces of his past began to spill out. We compared stories about our exes, as if swapping scars counted as intimacy.

At one point, he asked if I had a boyfriend.

I told him yes, because technically, at that time, I did.

His name was Jesus.

But even as the words left my mouth, a whisper pressed against my spirit:

"This isn't what you want."

I ignored the whisper.

I watched Kai move through the world like a man raised on manners and Sunday-school charm. He wasn't just polite—he embodied politeness in a way that made everyone around him soften just a little.

He greeted every person we passed,

nodding respectfully,

smiling with that easy warmth he carried like a second skin.

And then came the moment that stayed with me.

We were approaching a set of double doors, and an elderly woman was making her way toward them—slow, steady, careful. Before I could react, Kai stepped ahead, reached for the handle, and held the door open with the kind of attentiveness you don't see often anymore.

Not rushed.

Not performative.

Just… right.

He stood tall, posture straight, eyes lowered respectfully as she walked through.

The woman paused halfway, turned back to look him directly in the face, and her expression softened the way only age and wisdom can soften a person.

"Thank you, young man," she said, her voice gentle and warm.

Kai smiled—small, genuine, almost boyish.

"Yes, ma'am," he replied. "You're welcome."

It was such a simple exchange,

so ordinary on the surface,

yet something about it tugged me.

Because in that moment, I saw the man he wanted the world to believe he was—

the gentleman,

the protector,

the respectful one,

the man who made strangers smile and old women bless him without being asked.

And I mirrored that courtesy in myself,

because kindness begets kindness,

and watching him move with such grace made me feel like I was standing next to someone who elevated the room just by entering it.

For a moment,

I let myself believe this was who he truly was.

The man who held doors open.

The man who softened his voice for elders.

The man who made goodness look effortless.

I didn't know yet that charm and character

are not the same thing.

That courtesy can be costume.

That a man can open doors for strangers

and still close the wrong ones in private.

But in that moment—

watching him smile at a grateful old woman—

my heart swelled with quiet admiration.

It wouldn't be the last time

I mistook politeness

for purity.

He was handsome.

He had a beautiful smile.

He was respectful.

He knew gospel songs I thought only the old saints remembered.

And when he talked about God, he made it sound like the two of them were on speaking terms—as if heaven whispered to him in a language I hadn't learned yet.

I was intrigued.

Drawn in.

My healing had made me soft, and he slipped right through that softness like water through open fingers.

Because that's what happens when a woman is recovering.

You're tender.

Open.

Relearning how to breathe.

Relearning how to hope.

And men like him know how to walk through the doors healing leaves unlocked.

We exchanged numbers.

Just small talk at first, casual, harmless, simple.

Then the phone calls started.

Long ones.

Late ones.

Ones that stretched into the night until my eyelids grew heavy and the sound of his voice felt familiar, comforting, almost ordained.

We laughed easily, the kind of laughter that comes when two people feel seen.

We shared stories—childhood memories, faith journeys, heartbreaks.

He asked me questions no man had ever cared to ask before.

And a part of me softened even more.

As if God Himself was stitching something between us.

We connected like two people who had known each other for years, not days.

And at the end of every late-night phone call,

right before we said goodnight,

Kai would pray a small prayer of covering over my life.

It didn't matter how tired he was,

how long the day had been,

or how late the hour stretched—he always made space for prayer.

His voice would soften, settle, wrap itself in a reverence that made my heart open without permission.

"Father, protect Angela tonight," he would whisper.

"Cover her mind.

Cover her rest.

Let Your angels watch over her while she sleeps."

Looking back, I realized it wasn't connection.

It was recognition—two wounded spirits sensing each other's broken places.

But at the time, it felt like alignment.

It felt like purpose.

It felt like... finally.

The next day Kai and I went on our first date. At the restaurant, we talked for hours.

Everything was light, warm, and familiar. It felt as if we were the only two people in the restaurant, even though the place was full and buzzing around us. His voice drowned out every other sound. His presence filled every corner of my awareness.

He had my undivided attention, and he was slowly winning my heart with his compassionate stories and his professed love for Christ. He shared memories of ministry, testimonies from the pulpit, and scriptures quoted with ease.

And I won't lie-

it was intriguing.

Disarming.

Almost intoxicating.

It felt like the beginning of something promising.

As if God Himself had finally handed me the blessing I'd been patient enough to wait for.

Little did I know...

Every bit of that warmth was crafted.

Every part of that connection was curated.

The man singing gospel songs in the backseat… was a mask.

The stories he shared… were rehearsed.

The spirituality he showcased… was borrowed.

The persona he wore… was a costume. And I, a woman still tenders from healing, didn't yet know how to spot the difference between authenticity and performance.

CHAPTER TWO: The Night the Music Lied

Opening Lesson: *When the rhythm of someone's actions doesn't match their words, trust the rhythm.*

Healing makes you careful.

It makes you selective.

It makes you slow down when your spirit says, "Wait."

But sometimes the very thing you're healing from becomes the thing you unknowingly walk right back toward — wrapped in a different package, wearing a different smile, humming a different song.

That night started like so many others during that season of my life: quiet, low-lit, and filled with the soft hum of music floating through my apartment. Music has always been my escape. I collected songs the way some women collect perfume bottles — each one holding a memory, a mood, a moment of who I once was.

He came over, and it felt innocent.

Easy.

Comfortable.

We discovered early on that we both loved music and not just as background noise, but as a language. He knew lyrics from the old-school greats, those songs my parents played on Saturday mornings while cleaning the house. Songs that felt like heritage.

Back then, burning CDs was a thing and LimeWire was still alive, and playlists were curated with intention. We would sit for hours listening to old tracks, laughing, talking about the stories behind the songs. It felt like something out of a movie, the kind of connection people dream about.

Looking back, that was his first tactic:

1. Use what you love to make you feel safe.

That night, while the Isley Brothers Voyage to Atlantis played in the background, this song set the tone for the evening and made both of us comfortable. So comfortable too when Kai looked at me and spoke

"Hey... let's be intimate."

Just like that.

Soft.

Simple.

No hesitation in Kai's voice—only confidence, the kind that sounds like certainty.

And I agreed.

Not because I was reckless.

Not because I was desperate or lonely.

But because something about Kai's charm slipped past my defenses with ease.

He walked straight into a room I thought I had locked—

a room I had promised myself no man would enter again without covenant.

But healing can make your heart tender, and tenderness can blur the line between discernment and desire.

I'll be honest

I didn't expect much.

I assumed the sex would be ordinary, maybe even forgettable.

But what happened surprised me.

Kai seemed to know my body without instruction.

He knew where to touch, how to move, what to say to quiet my thoughts.

He created an atmosphere—attentive, gentle, almost studied.

Everything felt intentional, calculated but comforting.

It was as if Kai had rehearsed the entire moment,

as if he had memorized a script designed to make me feel chosen,

seen,

safe.

He moved toward me with an intention I didn't recognize then—half a man wanting to impress me, half a man determined to carve himself into my memory. His touch was careful, almost reverent, like he was learning a language he planned to speak fluently later.

And the truth?

It was amazing.

Not just in the way bodies usually collide and call it chemistry, but in a way that felt deeper—almost spiritual. There was closeness in the room, something warm and unfamiliar, something that made me feel like maybe, just maybe, I was stepping into a beginning rather than just a moment.

For the first time since my last heartbreak, I felt someone reaching a part of me I had kept closed for so long.

But looking back, I know this now:

Some men study your body so they can access your soul.

Some men create intimacy as a doorway, not a destination.

And some men learn your softness only to weaponize it later.

Back then, though, all I felt was warmth.

A dangerous warmth.

It softened me.

Opened me.

Invited me deeper into a story I didn't yet know I was stepping into blind.

Because while Kai had my body responding to him, responding beautifully, my spirit stayed still. Detached. Watching. There was a subtle disconnection inside me, a quiet whisper that rose like a soft warning from the deepest part of myself:

Don't give all of yourself. Not to him.

But the moment glowed warmly around us.

The room breathed softly.

The illusion felt comforting.

And I was a woman relearning her own touch, her own desire, her own aliveness.

So, I ignored it.

And when it was over, Kai did something no man had ever done before.

He didn't roll away.

He didn't sink into silence.

He didn't ask the usual questions that turned intimacy into a performance review.

Instead, he looked at merely and asked gently:

"Did I please you?"

"Did anything feel uncomfortable?"

"How was that for you?"

It was the first moment I felt the story bend... not toward love, but toward something far more complicated.

Questions meant to sound caring.

Questions meant to feel intimate.

But questions can also be tools when placed in the wrong hands.

Kai left that morning and before he walked out the door, he gave me a gentle kiss on the forehead and said goodbye. I didn't call him, but my mind was still on what we shared.

Partly because I was still processing what happened,

partly because my spirit felt unsettled,

and partly because something deep in my chest whispered:

"You opened Pandora's box."

On the way to work, I picked up my friend Keisha—the same friend who had been nudging, hinting, orchestrating us from day one. She slid into the passenger seat with a grin so bright it felt like it could split the sky open.

"What happened last night?" she asked, already laughing.
"You had sex with him, didn't you?"

My hands tightened on the steering wheel.
How did she know?
Was it written all over my face?
Was I glowing? Was I guilty?

Her excitement swept us back into a younger version of ourselves—two girls in a parked car, whispering, giggling, sharing secrets we had no business celebrating but always did anyway.

I didn't deny it.
I didn't have to.

Keisha squealed, kicking her feet like joy was something that needed to escape her body. And then, just when the moment felt harmless and sweet, she said something I still remember with unsettling clarity.

"I asked him if he talked to you today…"
She dragged the words out, savoring the suspense.
"And he smiled and said, 'Well, I have a new friend.'"

A new friend.

The words hit the air with a dull thud, flattening the warmth in my chest.

Not a woman he respected.

Not someone he cherished.

Not a connection he held carefully in both hands.

Just a new friend—spoken with the kind of boyish pride that made my stomach twist.

Because it wasn't pride.

It was possession.

A chill crawled up my spine, quiet but certain.

That wasn't romance.

That was ownership disguised as charm.

But I didn't know that yet—not fully, not consciously.

I was still letting the warmth convince me I was safe.

We pulled into the parking lot at work, still laughing, still replaying the night before as though joy could drown out intuition. My phone buzzed the moment I shifted into park.

Kai.

His name lit up my screen, and for a heartbeat, everything inside me went perfectly still.

I answered, breath caught between hope and apprehension.

The first words out of Kai's mouth were—

"Why haven't you called me?"

Not *How are you?*

Not *Good morning.*

Not even *Did you sleep well?*

Just a question designed to put me on the defensive.

At the time, I didn't see it for what it was

a control tactic disguised as concern.

So, I apologized.

I explained myself.

I softened my tone, like a woman who thought she owed him something.

"I didn't call because I thought you might be asleep… or busy."

He let me talk.

He didn't interrupt.

He absorbed every word.

And once he heard what he needed — my guilt, my eagerness to please, my openness to being corrected — he shifted right back into the man from the night before.

Warm.

Gentle.

Reassuring.

"We'll talk later," he said softly.

"Have a blessed day."

Looking back, everything about that moment flashes like a red warning light.

But at that time in my life, it felt like attention.

It felt like connection.

It felt like the next step in something promising.

I didn't realize the music, the warmth, the tenderness, and even the intimacy were carefully crafted tools.

I didn't know I had stepped into the beginning of a story that would break me…

only so I could learn how to build myself stronger.

CHAPTER THREE: The Fault Line Beneath the Fantasy

Opening Lesson: *What shatters the fantasy often reveals the truth you were never meant to ignore.*

Life has a way of piling things onto you so slowly, so quietly, that you don't realize how much weight you're carrying until your knees begin to tremble under it. By the time this man stepped into my life, I was already balancing more than I had ever admitted out loud.

A high-pressure sales job.

Six-day workweeks.

A toxic environment that drained me long before the clock hit five.

College courses I squeezed into every leftover minute.

Tuition paid out of pocket.

Long hours.

Lost sleep.

New friendships that needed tending.

And now... a new relationship I never saw coming.

I was stretched thin, a woman made of ambition and fatigue, holding herself together with coffee, deadlines, and sheer determination. And he slipped into the cracks of my exhaustion so easily—like water finding dry soil.

Like someone drawn to the silence between my breaths.

Like someone who recognized a woman trying to be strong while quietly unraveling.

And the truth is, when you're exhausted, even the wrong person can feel relief.

Not because they soothe you.

Not because they fill your empty spaces with gentleness.

But because they take root while you're too tired to notice the planting.

My grades began to slip.

My focus drifted.

The sharpness that once defined me softened into a haze.

I began rearranging my schedule around him without ever consciously deciding to. Little shifts at first—five minutes here, ten minutes there—but exhaustion makes decisions for you.

And charm?

Charm can disguise almost anything.

Because when you're worn thin, even chaos can feel like comfort if it's wrapped in attention and sweetness and the illusion of care.

And that's exactly how he entered my life—not as a storm, not as a warning, but as a warm breeze on a tired day.

Soft enough to welcome.

Strong enough to change everything.

The Vacation That Changed Everything

One day, my close friend Keisha suggested we take a trip—a couple's cruise to Mexico.

Something fun.

Something new.

Something that might shake the weight off our shoulders and remind us what it felt like to breathe without pressure.

"You can bring him," Keisha said, nudging me with a grin.

"He needs a vacation too."

It sounded harmless. Hopeful. Like a chance to reset my life and maybe my heart.

So I mentioned it to Kai casually, not expecting anything more than a polite shrug.

But his response was instant.

"I would love to go. I've always wanted to take a trip like that."

The excitement in his voice softened me.

His eagerness felt like alignment, like we were stepping into something real, something mutual.

For a moment it felt like confirmation, like God was smiling on this new chapter I was trying to build.

Then came the thread that would eventually unravel everything:

He mentioned he didn't have the money.

And I didn't even hesitate.

The healer in me stepped forward—the giver, the nurturer, the woman who picked people up even when her own knees were shaking.

"Don't worry about it," I told him.

"I'll pay for your part."

And just like that, I took responsibility for his presence in a place where he showed no ability—or intention—to enter on his own.

A pattern I didn't yet recognize...
but one that would echo again through our story.

Generosity has always been my love language, and he knew exactly how to respond to it. He acted grateful—so grateful that I convinced myself I was doing the right thing, being the right woman.

We spent more money on outfits than we spent on the cruise itself.
Matching clothes.
New shoes.
Planning the excursions, the dinners, the moments.

I laid out a future in color-coded Pinterest dreams while he simply stepped into the spaces I paid for.

But at the time, I didn't see the imbalance.
I only saw togetherness.
I only saw potential.
I only saw what I hoped love could become.

It felt like a dream.

The Spiritual Cracks Begin to Show

By the time we boarded the ship, my spirit was louder than my mind.

I had been deep in prayer during that season—raw, sensitive, emotionally open in a way that made the world feel brighter and heavier at the same time. Anything could trigger a worship moment back then. A lyric. A memory. Even a sudden quiet. I would slip into prayer the way some people slip into sleep.

So, when we settled into the small cabin we were sharing, and praise music played from the little radio we'd packed, something in me responded. The spirit of worship wrapped around me like a warm cloth I couldn't remove.

I knew I was on vacation.

I knew I was supposed to be relaxing, unwinding, having fun.

But the Holy Spirit doesn't wait for convenience. And I felt Him.

Kai sat quietly on the edge of the bed while I stood in the center of the room, eyes closed, hands lifted, voice trembling as I called on the name of Jesus.

He didn't mock me.

He didn't interrupt.

He didn't sigh or scroll through his phone or shift impatiently.

He just watched—his back half-turned toward the ocean view window, his face unreadable, his posture perfectly still.

At the time, I interpreted that as respect.

As support.

As evidence that he cared for the parts of me that weren't physical, weren't playful, weren't simple.

But now?

Now I understand it differently.

A man who wants to manipulate you will study what feeds you spiritually—not so he can feed you, but so he can mimic the source.

And Kai studied me that day.

He studied my worship.

He studied my surrender.

He studied the way my spirit moved when I was connected to God.

Even on that cruise, far from the noise of home, my spirit felt heavy—like it knew something my heart wasn't ready to accept.

And when the spirit is uneasy...

the body always follows.

The Confrontation in Mexico

The turning point came in Mexico.

The sun was bright, the air warm, laughter everywhere—vacation energy. But beneath all of it, something unseen was shifting. Something my spirit had been whispering about since before we left shore.

It started with something small.

So small it shouldn't have mattered.

A pack of cigarettes or something just as insignificant.

Keisha pulled me aside, her face tight with confusion.

"Girl… I think Kai stole something from the store on the ship."

It sounded ridiculous.

Out of character for the man he presented himself to be.

Embarrassing, even, to repeat.

But the moment she said it, something inside me, that same spirit that had felt heavy for days stirred. I approached him gently, softly, the way you approach an injury you're not sure is real. "Did you steal that item… a pack of cigarettes or something from the store?" I asked. My voice barely above a whisper. "They told me you took something, and I wanted to make sure it wasn't true."

He turned to me sharply, irritation already written across his face.

"No. Where did you get that from?" His voice wasn't loud, but it had an edge — sharp, defensive.

"I'm just saying what they—"

I didn't even finish the sentence before he stormed off.

Not walked.

Not clarified.

Stormed.

Straight toward the same friends who had mentioned it.

Straight into the open space where everyone was gathered.

And right there, with the sun hitting his face and tourists passing by, he confronted Keisha and her date.

"Did you tell Angela I stole something?"

The air thickened instantly.

People turned.

Voices fell quiet.

Keisha's eyes widened, stunned and offended.

Her date shifted awkwardly, unsure whether to step in or step back.

My heart dropped to my stomach.

Not because of the accusation.

Not even because of the possibility that it might be true.

But because of the explosion.

The speed.

The intensity.

It was the first time I saw the mask slip—

the first time I saw anger move through him like it had been waiting for an opportunity.

And in that moment, beneath the heat and the noise and the confusion…

my spirit whispered again.

Pay attention.

This is the real him.

This is the moment you cannot ignore.

The humiliating part?

They lied.

Both of them.

They looked me straight in my face and said they never told me anything.

As if my discernment was flawed.

As if my memory couldn't be trusted.

As if the intuition God gave me was somehow broken.

And instead of pulling me aside...

instead of clarifying gently...

instead of protecting my dignity...

Kai confronted me in front of everyone.

His voice.

His posture.

His anger.

It was the first time I felt something inside me shift—

the first crack in the fantasy,

the first glimpse of the man behind the mask.

And right there, beneath the noise of Mexico and the heat of the sun, my spirit whispered again:

"This is not what you want."

But whispers are easy to silence when you're still trying to convince yourself that a burden is a blessing.

His tone was sharp.

His words were cutting.

His eyes were cold.

In seconds, everything warm about him evaporated.

The tenderness.

The charm.

The softness he had used to win me over.

All of it vanished.

And I felt small.

Embarrassed.

Exposed.

Like I had stepped into the light only to discover someone else had control of the switch.

Like maybe I had imagined the entire conversation that led us here.

Like maybe *I* was the problem.

So, I did the only thing my spirit allowed in that moment—

I stepped back.

Not physically.

Spiritually.

Emotionally.

Just enough to breathe.

Just enough to see him clearly. Shortly after I returned to the cruise ship,

eyes swollen from crying,

heart still pounding from the walk back,

the phone in our cabin rang.

The sound startled me—

sharp, intrusive, too loud for my fragile state of mind.

I picked it up with trembling hands.

"Hello?"

A calm voice on the other end asked,

"Ma'am, are you in the room alone? Has Mr. Turner returned yet?"

I wiped my face quickly, embarrassed even though they couldn't see me.

"No," I said softly.

"He hasn't returned yet…

but I'm sure they're on their way back."

The call ended politely, and the room fell silent again. And that phone call gave me a weird feeling.

A few minutes later, the door opened.

Kai walked in.

He didn't storm in this time.

He didn't yell.

He didn't look angry.

If anything, he looked… composed.

Calculated.

Prepared.

He sat down on the edge of the bed—the same way he always did when he needed me to listen, not question.

He looked at me with this expression that almost mimicked concern.

"I know you're upset," he said softly.

"But I had to confront them."

I didn't say anything.

I just stared, waiting.

"I don't hold things back," he continued.

"I'm not like other people. I don't talk behind people's backs. I confront them to their face. That's the kind of man I am."

He shook his head, frustrated—

but not with himself.

"With them," he said.

"This is what they do.

They lie.

They always lie.

I asked them directly and look how they acted.

You saw it."

He shifted everything—

every ounce of blame,

every ounce of embarrassment,

every ounce of accountability—

away from himself and onto them.

He never apologized for exploding.

Never acknowledged the scene he caused.

Never mentioned how humiliated I felt.

He just kept redirecting my pain

away from his actions

and toward someone else.

And because I was exhausted...

because I was emotionally drained...

because I wanted peace more than I wanted truth...

I believed him.

I believed his tone.

His confidence.

His certainty.

His explanations sounded so righteous, so logical, so convincing.

I believed him

because I wanted to—

because believing him felt easier

than confronting the possibility

that the man I cared for

was the one causing all my hurt.

I didn't recognize it then,

but that moment—

sitting in a dim cabin on a ship in Mexico—

wasn't closure.

It was conditioning.

The Morning After

I jumped out of my sleep to the sound of keys rattling.

Not gently.

Not by accident.

Metal scraped against the lock, deliberate, searching, as if someone was trying to figure out whether the door would give. My heart slammed as I pushed myself upright, the dim cabin still heavy with the remnants of sleep. For a split second, I didn't know where I was—only that something was wrong.

The keys rattled again.

Then came the knock.

Hard. Final.

"Security. Open the door."

Kai froze beside me. I felt my breath catch, the air in the cabin thickening until it was hard to inhale. He moved slowly, carefully, as if sudden motion might make things worse, and cracked the door open.

Two officers stepped inside.

The first was tall, his presence calm but commanding, the kind of calm that made the room feel smaller. The second was younger, sharp-eyed, alert—his gaze already scanning, already measuring. The taller officer looked between us, unhurried, assessing, like he was reading a story we hadn't finished telling.

"Good morning," he said evenly. "We need to verify the identity of everyone in this cabin."

Kai's voice softened instantly—the same tone he used in the beginning, the one that once felt reassuring.

"Is something wrong, sir?"

The younger officer didn't respond to the question. Instead, he spoke like someone who wasn't interested in explanations.

"As part of docking protocol, customs run every passenger's name."

He paused, letting the silence stretch, letting the weight of his words settle into the room.

Then he looked directly at Kai.

"Your name," he said, his eyes narrowing, "flagged in the system."

The air left my lungs. My stomach twisted before I even knew why—instinct reacted faster than thought.

Kai tried to smile. He tried to charm it away. Tried to smooth the moment into something harmless.

"There must be a mistake," he said, almost laughing.

But the taller officer didn't move. Didn't blink. Didn't soften.

He simply lifted the folder in his hand and opened it.

And at that moment, I knew—whatever was inside had already crossed the threshold.

I didn't know the man I had prayed for.

Not at all.

After the officers left and the room fell quiet again, I sat frozen on the edge of the bed, staring at the door Kai had just been taken through.

My mind was racing, but my body felt numb.

I needed air.

I needed answers.

I needed… someone who knew me.

So, I stood up, wiped my face, and walked out of my cabin and into the hallway.

The hallway felt longer than usual, filled with people who had no idea my world had just cracked open. Every laugh, every suitcase rolling across the carpet, every cheerful voice felt painfully out of place.

I made my way to Keisha's cabin, heart pounding so hard I could feel it in my throat.

I knocked.

Once.

Twice.

Finally, the door opened, and Keisha appeared — hair wrapped, eyes still sleepy but instantly alert when she saw my face.

"Angela... what's wrong?"

I stepped inside, and the words spilled out of me in fragments.

"They arrested him."

Keisha's eyes widened.

"What?" Who? Kai?!"

I nodded, my voice trembling.

"Yes... the officers came to our room. Customs ran his name, and... he has a felony warrant."

Her hand shot up to her mouth.

"Oh my God."

I paced the small space, trying to catch my breath, trying to make sense of something that didn't make sense at all.

"They took him," I said, gesturing helplessly. "Right there in front of me. Cuffed him. Walked him out."

Keisha sat down slowly, shocked settling over her.

"Angela... I don't even know what to say."

Neither did I.

Because how do you explain being blindsided?

How do you explain the slow unraveling of a man you thought God sent?

How do you explain that the whisper in your spirit had been right all along?

I sank into a chair.

"I don't know him, Keisha," I whispered.

"I don't know anything about him."

Keisha reached for my hand, squeezing it gently.

"We're getting off this ship soon. You don't have to deal with this alone."

But even surrounded by friends...

I felt alone.

Because humiliation can isolate you.

Shock can silence you.

And betrayal — the kind wrapped in charm, gospel music, and soft-spoken promises — can turn the whole world into a blur.

I looked toward the cabin door, the hallway beyond it, the ship that was now just holding the remnants of a fantasy I didn't ask for.

"I just want to go home," I said softly.

And for the first time all trip,

I meant it with every part of me.

Kai's One Free Phone Call

Later that afternoon, my phone rang — an unknown number.

I already knew.

I answered anyway.

"Hello?"

A pause.

A breath.

Then:

"Angela... it's me."

Kai.

His voice was soft, strained, carefully arranged—like someone trying to sound broken without being broken.

"I didn't do what they're saying," he insisted quickly. "This is just a misunderstanding."

I closed my eyes.

"Kai, customs said there's a felony warrant," I said quietly. "They don't arrest people for misunderstandings."

He danced around the truth.

Dodging.

Minimizing.

Deflecting.

"It's old stuff," he said. "Stuff from years ago. I didn't even know it was still active. You *must* believe me."

But for the first time since meeting him, I heard the difference between sincerity and strategy.

"Why didn't you tell me?" I asked.

Silence stretched across the line.

Then he whispered the sentence manipulators use like clockwork:

"I didn't want you to judge me. I need you, Angela. Don't give up on me."

A robotic voice cut in:

"You have thirty seconds remaining."

He panicked.

"Just don't leave me. Please. Please. Don't leave me."

But even through the static, I could hear it
he didn't call to apologize.
He didn't call to check on me.
He didn't call to make things right.

He called to secure his position
even from a jail cell.

And because I was still the woman who fixed things, the woman who carried more than her share, the woman who kept showing up even when she was tired…

I heard myself saying,

"We are on the way to bond you out of there. Just sit tight."

The line disconnected.

The Truth Revealed

When he was finally released, he walked toward me with that same practiced calm, that same controlled face, and looked at me dead in my eyes.

"I need an attorney."

No apology.

No accountability.

No remorse.

Just need.

Always need.

Always *taking*.

And that's when the truth came out:

The arrest warrant was for burglary.

Not a misunderstanding.

Not a paperwork error.

Not an old, harmless mistake.

Burglary.

A crime of intrusion.

A crime of taking what didn't belong to him.

And as soon as I heard it, something in my spirit clicked.

He hadn't just taken from stores.

Or from people.

Or from places he had no right to be.

He had taken from me.

My peace.

My time.

My energy.

My trust.

And I finally understood the pattern:

A man who will steal with his hands

will steal with his presence.

With his charm.

With his need.

With his silence.

With his lies.

And I had been robbed long before customs intervened.

Burglary.

A minister.

A man of God.

A preacher.

Charged with burglary.

I couldn't believe it.

I didn't *want* to believe it.

The man I was falling for was not a blessing

he was a lesson.

And that was only the beginning.

Layer by layer,

truth by truth,

lie by lie,

he revealed himself.

But before I could escape him...

before I could see clearly...

before the mask fully shattered...

I had to walk through hell and back.

And at this moment

this unraveling

was only the doorway.

CHAPTER FOUR: When God Pulled Back the Curtain

Opened Lesson: When *God reveals the truth, it rarely feels like protection at first sometimes it feels like heartbreak.*

There comes a point in every storm where the rain gets so heavy,

you can't tell whether God is trying to drown you

or cleanse you.

During that season,

I didn't know the difference.

Everything after his arrest became a blur—

a whirlwind I never saw coming,

a storm I never asked to weather.

Life shifted almost overnight into a cycle of:

- court hearings
- legal paperwork
- missed work shifts
- attorney fees
- emotional chaos
- and a spiritual heaviness I couldn't pray away

And in the middle of all that weight, all that unraveling,

there was one morning that still clings to me with a strange mixture of ache and confusion.

The Prayer Before Court-Kai and Angela

We were parked outside the courthouse,

the sun barely rising,

casting long shadows across the dashboard.

Kai sat beside me, breathing too hard,

fidgeting with the sleeves of his shirt,

his knee bouncing in quiet panic.

He wouldn't admit fear,

but fear was sitting right there in the space between us.

He reached for my hand.

Not gently—urgently.

Like someone grasping for the only lifeline they had left.

"Angela… before we go in," he whispered,

"can we pray? Please. I need it. I need God right now."

His voice cracked in a way that made my heart tug against its own warning.

Kai bowed his head, and for a moment,

He looked humble.

He looked repentant.

He looked like the man I prayed he could become.

Then he began:

"Father God...

I come to You because I don't have anybody else right now.

I know I made mistakes—

mistakes I'm not proud of.

But Lord, You said in Your Word

that You look at the heart,

not the past.

And You know my heart.

You know I'm trying.

You know I'm changing.

Cover me in Your mercy today.

Let Your favor fall in that courtroom.

Let the judge see the man I'm trying to be,

not the man I was.

And Lord..."

he squeezed my hand harder,

voice trembling as if he'd practiced the break,

"...bless Angela.

She is the woman you sent to stand by me.

Give her strength to hold me up

when I can't hold myself.

Give her peace about our future.

Let nothing come between us—

not fear, not people, not lies, not misunderstanding.

Protect us, God.

Protect what we're building.

Don't let this situation destroy the plans You have for us.

We need You.

I need You.

I need *her*.

And I'm trusting you to bring me out of this."

He ended with a long, shaky exhale,

lifting his eyes to mine as if waiting

for absolution.

And for a moment...

I believed every word.

The sincerity.

The brokenness.

The divine language.

The way he intertwined God with "our future."

I didn't yet understand that some prayers

aren't about reaching heaven—

they're about reaching the person sitting beside you.

I whispered my own prayer under my breath:

"God... show me the truth."

And He did.

Just not gentle.

The Spiritual Battle

I wasn't just confused.

I wasn't just heartbroken.

I was wrestling—

spiritually, emotionally, mentally—

trying to reconcile the God I trusted

with the man He had allowed into my life.

Kai didn't just break my trust.

He broke the image I had built of him—

the one I called divine,

the one I mistook for answered prayer,

the one I believed held purpose.

But when God pulls back the curtain,

He doesn't do it softly.

He does it in a way that forces you to confront truth:

- Not everyone who calls His name belongs to Him.
- Not everyone who quotes scripture carries His Spirit
- Not everyone who prays with you is praying for you.

And I was about to learn that lesson

one heartbreak at a time.

Because I was still trying to reconcile the man who prayed passionately with me in that car...

with the man who had a warrant for burglary.

The Courtroom Spiral

Attorney Marcus Ellison was the kind of lawyer you hired when you didn't have the money, but you still needed someone to stand beside you in court.

He was tall, wiry, with deep-set eyes that looked permanently tired — like life had wrung him out a long time ago. His suit never quite fit, his tie was always slightly crooked, and his briefcase looked older than both of us combined.

But his demeanor was steady.

Calm.

Almost numb from years of handling cases heavier than the people who carried them.

He never sugarcoated anything.

He never raised his voice.

He never seemed shocked.

He just sat there with his pen tapping lightly against his legal pad as he explained the charges, his tone clinical, detached — as if he were discussing the weather and not the possibility of a man's life collapsing.

"The prosecution is seeking twenty years," he said matter-of-factly, adjusting his glasses that constantly slid down his nose.

Kai's breath caught.

Twenty years.

When we left Attorney Ellison's office that day, Kai was shaking.

Later that night, he looked at me with fear I had never seen before. His voice cracked as he said,

"Angela… I can't do twenty years in prison. If I'm convicted and locked away that long… I'll kill myself."

The words dropped between us like a stone.

Heavy.

Dark.

Terrifying.

For a moment, the world felt painful still.

This was the same man who preached to me, quoted scripture,

sang gospel songs with conviction,

and claimed God spoke through him.

Yet now he was speaking death over himself.

I stared at him, overwhelmed, and asked softly,

"Where is your faith?"

The question wasn't judgment.

It was desperation.

A plea.

Because the man who told *me* to trust God

was now unraveling in front of me.

But instead of anchoring himself,

instead of reaching for God,

instead of finding strength...

Kai spiraled deeper into fear.

And without realizing it,

I started carrying the weight of his fear as if it were my own.

A burden no woman should bear.

A burden I was never equipped to hold.

A burden that would slowly wrap itself around every corner of my life

I fought for him like I was fighting for air.

I slipped into "fixer mode"—a dangerous place where love becomes duty and duty becomes self-destruction.

The Other Woman

All the while, the streets and eventually the office began to whisper.

The woman he was accused of stealing from wasn't the only woman in the picture.

There was another.

A younger woman.

A coworker.

A girl living a life completely opposite from mine.

Her name was **Tiana Reed**.

Tiana was the kind of girl who entered a room like a storm—loud, bold, unpredictable.

Pretty, but in a reckless, unrestrained kind of way.

Hair colors that changed with her moods.

Eyelashes dramatic enough to cast shadows.

Clothes that hugged every curve like she needed validation with every step.

She lived in chaos the way some people live in harmony—

drama, late nights, impulsive choices, alcohol-fueled emotions, and men who fed off instability.

But what made her story even more heartbreaking was this:

Tiana had a calling on her life.

A real one.

A ministry anointing that was obvious to anyone with spiritual eyes.

But she was running from it.

Running hard.

Running fast.

Everything about her life looked like rebellion against a gift she didn't want to carry.

You could see the tension in her —

the war between who she was created to be

and who she was choosing to become.

She and I were nothing alike.

I was steady.

She was scattered.

I was rooted.

She was drifting.

I was running toward God.

She was running away from Him.

But in some twisted way, we were the same.

We were both clinging to a man who belonged to neither of us.

A man who fed on our insecurity, our softness, our broken places.

And Kai?

He played us against each other like puppets on strings.

Everyone at work knew.

Everyone gossiped.

Everyone laughed.

The church girl.

The good one.

The perfect one.

Caught in a scandal she never asked for.

Tiana's taunting didn't stop.

Her arrogance grew, fueled by the attention she received and the drama she seemed to crave.

And my heart—already fragile.

began to crack under pressure.

A pressure born from betrayal, comparison, confusion, and a spiritual battle neither of us realized we were fighting.

The Confrontation — But Not the First One

It didn't happen the first time Tiana smirked at me.

Or the second.

Or even the third.

By then, her little games felt almost predictable—

the whispers, the side comments, the dramatic eyerolls she thought were intimidating. She played mean girl like it was a personality trait, not realizing it only exposed how young she really was inside.

But one afternoon, after weeks of her childish taunting, I walked into the break room and found Tiana standing there alone. She turned toward me with that same tired smirk—

the one meant to get a reaction she never earned.

"Angela," she said, folding her arms, "you really think you're the only one he talks to?"

Her tone was sharp, but her spirit was flimsy.

Her whole aura screamed insecurity dressed up as attitude.

I didn't flinch.

I didn't shrink.

I didn't let her pull me into her playground of immaturity.

Instead, I took a breath, straightened my shoulders, and met her gaze with a calm she couldn't touch.

"Tiana," I said softly, "you've got a child's understanding of grown folks' business."

Her smile faltered.

"You keep poking at something you know nothing about. If you spent half the time working on your own life that you spend worrying about mine, you might feel secure."

She scoffed. "Girl, please. He told me—"

I held up a hand.

Firm.

Unbothered.

In control.

"Stop. You sound silly."

Her eyes widened, offended.

"You want the truth?" I asked, tilting my head slightly.

"Here it is Kai is in love with me."

Tiana blinked.

The smirk faded completely.

"He chose *me*," I continued.

"And not only that"

I let a slow, but confident smile.

"we're getting married soon."

Her mouth dropped open.

"You're lying," she whispered.

"No," I said, my voice steady as stone. "You just can't handle that someone sees in me what you're still searching for in yourself."

She looked away then—

not out of disinterest,

but because the truth stung deeper than she expected.

"You don't need to insert yourself into our relationship," I added.

"Kai and I are building a future. A real one. Something your childish games can't touch."

The room felt different than quiet, grounded, settled.

Like she finally realized she'd been playing checkers while I'd been living a whole life, she knew nothing about.

"Stay out of grown folks' business, Tiana," I said calmly as I walked past her.

"And stop embarrassing yourself."

She didn't follow me.

She didn't speak again.

She just stood there—

a little girl in grown woman makeup,

finally realizing she'd picked the wrong one to provoke.

Tiana didn't have a comeback.

Just silence.

The silence so heavy it felt like it settled on her shoulders first,

then the room,

then mine.

And for the first time in a long time,

I felt **good**.

Good for saying what I needed to say.

Good for matching her energy with something sharper and wiser.

Good for finally giving her a piece of my mind—

even if a piece of it was dressed in a lie.

Because whether Kai was in love with me...

whether or not marriage was ever in our cards...

Tiana needed to hear something that would make her step back,

grow up,

and stop inserting herself into things that had nothing to do with her.

And I needed to feel what it was like to defend myself

instead of shrinking under someone else's insecurity.

But as the silence stretched between us,

as her eyes dropped for the first time,

as her smirk dissolved into nothing—

I realized something deeper:

Kai wasn't choosing between us.

There was never a competition.

He wasn't lifting one of us while rejecting the other.

He was using both of us in different ways.

And the spiritual battle I thought I was fighting?

It wasn't between me and Tiana at all.

It was between **truth and deception**.

Purpose and distraction.

Calling and chaos.

That small confrontation wasn't loud.

It wasn't physical.

It wasn't dramatic.

But it was the **first time I stood up for myself**—

not to win a man,

not to prove a point,

but to reclaim a part of me I had been shrinking,

dimming,

quieting.

And in that still, quiet moment—

as Tiana stood there speechless

and I finally felt my spine straighten—

God pulled the curtain back just a little more.

Enough for me to see that strength doesn't always roar.

Sometimes it speaks softly,

truthfully,

strategically—

and then walks away with dignity.

The Sentence

After months of hearings and negotiations, the attorney came back with a plea:

Two years of probation

I exhaled like I hadn't breathed in months.

I cried.

I thanked God.

I thought we were finally free.

He wasn't relieved, not truly.

He was angry.

Probation wasn't his mercy

it was his exposure.

And God was slowly pulling back the curtain

on a truth I had been refusing to face:

A man who refuses to fight for himself

will destroy everyone who tries to save him.

But there was something even darker beneath the surface

spiritual manipulation.

Because every time Kai felt the consequences of his own actions,

he wrapped them in scripture,

twisted them into prophecy,

or disguised them as "attacks from the enemy."

He used God's name as a shield for his choices

and as a leash for my loyalty.

And that was the part I didn't recognize at the time:

He wasn't just manipulating my emotions

he was manipulating my faith.

Using the God I loved

to bind me to a man I was never meant to follow.

It wasn't love.

It wasn't partnership.

It wasn't spiritual alignment.

It was deception,

dressed in worship language,

whispered in prayer tones,

wrapped in the illusion of destiny.

And spiritual manipulation cuts deeper than lies

because it doesn't just confuse your mind.

It attacks your discernment.

It dulls your intuition.

It makes you question the voice of God inside you.

I didn't know it then,

but I was fighting more than a man.

I was fighting a spirit that knew exactly

which of my vulnerabilities to touch.

And this—

this unraveling—

was only the beginning.

The Day the Truth Broke Me

One night, after yet another confrontation with Tiana—the younger woman at work—something inside me snapped.

I couldn't understand her boldness.

I couldn't understand why she felt so comfortable disrespecting me.

I couldn't understand why he seemed so connected to her, so invested in her chaos, so drawn to the very thing he claimed God had delivered him from.

None of it made sense.

Until one day, in prayer, I heard a clear, quiet voice—

not loud, not harsh, just *truth* slipping gently into the place where confusion had been sitting:

"You don't know what you're fighting."

And that's when the final layer of truth unraveled.

I learned what he had been hiding:

- bipolar disorder
- schizophrenia
- drug Addiction

Not managed.

Not treated.

Not acknowledged.

Not controlled.

Just buried beneath charm, spirituality, manipulation, and emotional outbursts.

And suddenly, everything made sense:

The mood swings.

The spiritual language used out of context.

The chaos he left in every room he entered.

The unpredictability.

The fixation on both women.

The grandiose claims about God.

The instability masquerading as "anointing."

I wasn't just loving a broken man.

I was battling disorders I never knew existed,

carrying trauma that wasn't mine,

and trying to heal wounds I didn't create.

The truth didn't just break me.

It **freed** me.

I heard it—not out loud, but clear.

Look up the marriage license.

I shook my head slightly, almost offended by the thought.

"Lord... what marriage license?" I whispered.

The question hung in the air, unanswered—until it wasn't.

Search Kai's name on the state marriage license website.

The words came again, firmer this time. Not rushed. Not angry. Just certain.

That wasn't something I would ever think to do.

It wasn't in my nature.

It wasn't in my mind.

It was a whisper from someplace holy—

a nudge from the same God who had been trying to warn me for months.

My hands trembled as I sat down at my computer.

I stared at the screen for a long moment,

heart pounding,

spirit bracing itself for something I couldn't name.

Then slowly,

carefully,

obediently...

I typed in his name.

And the screen lit up with truth:

He was married.

Legally.

Officially.

Fully.

His wife's name was **Monique Turner**.

A woman who had stood before God and the state with him.

A woman who likely endured storms I couldn't imagine.

A woman he never mentioned.

Not once.

Not even in passing.

My breath left my body.

The room went silent.

And every lie, every manipulation, every moment of confusion suddenly took shape:

I was never the only woman.

I was never the chosen woman.

I was the *other* woman—

without ever knowing it.

It wasn't just betrayal.

It was deception layered in scripture,

wrapped in charm,

delivered in prayer tones.

And God had to lead me

step by step,

whisper by whisper,

truth by truth...

to the revelation

I wasn't ready for

but desperately needed.

Confronting Kai

He came to my apartment that day—

unsuspecting,

unbothered,

confident in the lies he thought he'd buried deep.

He walked in like everything was normal.

But nothing was normal anymore.

I looked him straight in the eyes and asked:

"Is there something you forgot to tell me?"

He blinked.

Acted confused.

Tilted his head like he genuinely had no idea what I meant.

He played dumb—

a role he'd perfected.

So, I said it.

Slowly.

Clearly.

Without trembling.

"You're married.

Are you married to a Mrs. Monique Turner?"

Everything in him froze.

Not because he was ashamed.

Not because he felt guilty.

But because he knew the lie he'd been living had finally collapsed.

He didn't deny it.

He couldn't.

Instead, he shrugged and said,

"I don't look at it that way."

As if marriage was a perspective.

As if vows were optional.

As if dishonesty could be softened into misunderstanding.

And then—

like a true manipulator—

he blamed her.

He told me about an argument they had on their wedding day.

He said he walked out and never looked back.

He claimed they lived separate lives.

He painted himself as the victim in a marriage he had hidden from me.

When I asked if he planned to go back to her,

he said **no** without hesitation.

When I asked what it would take to divorce her,

he said:

"I'll leave her. I'll get a divorce.

I want to be with you."

And I believed him.

Not because I was naïve.

Not because I lacked discernment.

But because:

Love makes fools out of even the wise.

Hope can blind you when your heart is tired.

And healing can turn into hurting

when you let the wrong man hold your vulnerability.

Because Kai knew how I felt about adultery.

I had told him, in our late-night conversations, in the moments where guards were down

and honesty felt sacred.

I told him how strongly I stood against it.

How it was something I would never do.

How it went against my values, my faith, my very identity.

And still, he chose to disregard that.

He chose silence over honesty.

He chose to move forward without giving me the dignity of a choice.

I was never given the option to decide

whether I wanted to continue a relationship with a married man.

That decision was made for me—

by omission.

And that was the moment I understood:

what he called protection was control.

What he framed as love was deception.

God does not dwell where truth is withheld.

And in that painful clarity,

I wasn't being destroyed.

I was being rescued.

But the truth was also the only thing

that would save me.

The Man I Prayed For

"Father… I come to you tonight with a heart that is trembling.

I am confused, I am hurting, and I don't know what to believe.

Lord, I repent.

Even though I didn't know Kai was married,

I still ask for Your forgiveness for being connected to a man who belonged to someone else.

Wash me clean, God.

Cleanse my heart, my thoughts, my emotions.

You know I never wanted to be out of Your will."

"But Lord... I also need your help.

Kai said he was getting a divorce.

Kai told me he wasn't staying in that marriage.

Kai told me they were done.

And Father, I don't know what's true anymore.

I don't know what to hold onto.

I don't know if I'm supposed to walk away

or stand still and trust You to work things out."

"God... if Kai is the man you have for me,

if he is truly meant to be part of my future,

then I ask You to make the path clear.

Fix what needs fixing.

Heal what needs healing.

Guide him into truth.

Guide him into righteousness.

Let him walk upright before you.

Make him the man you called him to be—

a holy man of God,

a man of integrity,

a man of honesty,

a man who honors you in all things."

"I love him, Lord...

and I don't know if this love is from you

or from my own broken places.

So I'm asking you...

help me.

Help my heart.

Help my mind.

Help my spirit discern what is real.

Help me see whether this relationship is your will

or a distraction sent to break me."

"I surrender this situation to you.

I surrender Kai to you.

I surrender my confusion, my hope, my fears.

If this relationship is not from you, remove it gently.

But if it is from you,

then Father...

make it right.

Turn his heart toward you.

Turn his life around.

Break every lie.

Expose every deception.

Do whatever you must to bring truth to the surface."

"Lord, please...

don't let me be fooled.

Don't let me be lost.

Don't let me cling to someone who isn't mine

unless You Yourself make him mine in your perfect timing."

"I trust You, even though my heart is conflicted.

Help me hold onto you when I don't know how to hold onto anything else."

"In Jesus' name,

Amen."

CHAPTER FIVE: Why Leaving Was Not Simple

Opening Lesson: *Love becomes a trap the moment you must abandon yourself to hold it together.*

People outside always ask the same question:

"Why didn't you just leave?

But love doesn't work like a light switch.

Attachment doesn't turn off with logic.

Investment doesn't disappear because pain walked in.

By the time the truth began unraveling —the drugs, the lies, the women, the marriage, the felony —I was already in too deep.

Emotionally.

Financially,

Spiritually.

Mentally.

I had poured time, money, prayers, tears, and dreams into a man who kept handing me reasons to walk away — and yet my heart kept choosing to stay

Because somewhere in my mind, I believed:

"If I love him hard enough, he'll see my worth."

"If I stand by him long enough, he'll choose me."

"If I pray strong enough, God will fix him."

"If I sacrifice enough, he'll finally love me back."

What I didn't know then was that this wasn't love. This was bonding — trauma bonding — disguised as loyalty. And it held me hostage.

The Breaking Point that Didn't Break Me

New truth kept slipping through the cracks—truth I wasn't ready to face. Kai was a married man, a convicted felon, a habitual liar, a manipulator, a drug user, emotionally unstable, involved with multiple women, and spiritually dangerous. And still, I stayed, not because I didn't see the signs, but because somewhere along the journey he stopped being a man and became a mission, a project, a soul I believed I could save. When love mixes with compassion, compassion can quietly turn into captivity, and I was already bound. But the final blow—the one that should have sent me running—was the pregnancy. The girl from work, the same one who taunted me, mocked me, flaunted her connection to him like a victory, was six months pregnant with his child while he lay in my bed at night swearing there was nothing between them. Everyone at work knew but me; everyone whispered, snickered, and connected the dots except for the woman fasting and praying for his deliverance. But deep down, I knew—God had already tried to warn me.

Before anyone ever said a word, I dreamed **Tiana** was pregnant, repeatedly. Each dream carried a heaviness I couldn't explain, like my spirit was sounding alarms while my heart kept pressing the snooze button. I ignored the dreams. I ignored the whispers. I ignored the uneasiness curling itself around my discernment. And then one day, someone at work said, "Tiana is pregnant." And I felt nothing. Not because I didn't care, but because my spirit had already mourned what my mind refused to accept. The grief was old by the time reality arrived. Not to mention, I asked Kai about the rumors and of course he denied it.

Jamaica: The Last Illusion

Ironically, just as the truth about Kai was unraveling, we planned another trip—a do-over to Jamaica to cover the wounds from the disastrous cruise where he'd been arrested. In Jamaica, we walked the beaches as if we were whole, laughing as the waves chased our feet and swimming in the ocean like the water could wash away everything we refused to face. We even met another couple, carefree, the kind of people who made vacations feel lighter—and went on a jeep ride with them along the shoreline, wind whipping through our hair, pretending our lives weren't tangled in lies back home. One afternoon, we toured Rose Hall located in Montego Bay, Jamaica, once a slave plantation, and the view from the great house perched on the hill was breathtaking; the Jamaican air wrapped around us like something ancient and holy, making the moment feel more captivating than it truly was. But beauty can't heal betrayal. The sun doesn't fix lies. Ocean water doesn't wash away heartbreak. And the truth was waiting the moment we returned home—her rounded belly, her due date, and Kai's denial as he insisted the child wasn't his and promised a DNA test, as if denial could rewrite conception and lies could erase life.

He swore he hadn't touched her but lies have a short shelf life. When Tiana gave birth, the truth arrived with her newborn—the baby looked exactly like Kai, right down to the eyes and the shape of his smile, and she even named the child after him. And still... still, I stayed. When I learned she had delivered his baby, I told him, "I'm hurt, but the child is innocent. All I ask is that you be a man and take care of your responsibilities." Saying it felt like swallowing broken glass, but I meant every word; responsibility and forgiveness were stitched into my DNA. Kai agreed, and that agreement—simple, fragile, deceptive—is what kept me tethered when I should have run. Not because it was noble, but because his willingness made me feel needed again, made me feel like we were still "us," even though "us" had fractured long ago. It wasn't love. It was delusion wrapped in hope. I stayed not because he earned it, but because I didn't know how to stop loving someone I had sacrificed so much for. Leaving him would have meant admitting that everything I believed in, prayed for, fought for, and held onto was a lie—and at that time in my life, I wasn't ready to face that truth.

CHAPTER SIX: The Night the Windows Shattered

Opening Lesson: *The first violent moment is also the last moment you can pretend you're safe.*

There are moments in life when time feels like it's holding its breath — moments so sharp they carve themselves into the memory of your bones. That night, sitting in my car outside his mother's house, time wasn't breathing at all. It was waiting on me. Waiting for me to finally see what love was doing to me.

But the truth is: I had been blinded for years.

I stayed with a man who lied, cheated, and manipulated with the same ease that most people breathe. I stayed through the late-night stories, the unexplained disappearances, the whispered apologies, and the tears I cried into my pillow while he slept like a man without a conscience.

But the hardest truth to swallow — the one I refused to speak for years — was this:

I stayed because the little girl inside me was still searching for her father.

My father was an ordained minister. Imperfect, flawed, human — but he loved me fiercely. When he preached, he carried the Word like a torch. When he looked at me, I never questioned his love. That kind of security leaves fingerprints on the heart, and sometimes we go searching for it in people who only know how to imitate the shape of love, not the substance of it.

And this man...

The way he held a cigarette between his fingers, the way he talked about Scripture with conviction — even though he lived none of it — something about him mirrored pieces of my father. Not the good pieces, but familiar ones. And familiarity can feel like home even when its danger dressed in memory.

My friend used to say, "The devil has a file on you."

And that night, I learned just how deep that file went.

The Call

It was late, somewhere between exhaustion and routine. I had just finished a long shift at a new job, a job I started because I needed something of my own — money he couldn't control, space he couldn't invade. He called asking me to come over, and I said yes without thinking. Yes, was my habit. Yes, it was my loyalty. Yes, it was the chain I kept pretending was jewelry.

When I pulled up to his mother's house, he was stuffing his belongings into bags. He told me he was coming back to my place. I sat in the car waiting, mind numb, heart tired

What happened next cracked open everything I thought I knew.

The Confrontation-Tiana

Tiana car screeched into the driveway, blocking me in. She knew my car. She always knew. She was drunk — so drunk that her words swayed before her body did. Her kids were in the backseat watching chaos unfold like it was bedtime television.

She stumbled toward us, rage dripping off her like sweat.

"Where are you going?" Tiana demanded.

"I'm leaving," Kai said.

"No, you're not," she spat. "You're coming with me!"

He got into my passenger seat, and she pounded her fists on the window — screaming, crying, daring him to move. I feared she'd break the glass and cut herself, so I cracked the window. The moment the space opened, she reached inside and punched him square in the face.

Still, he didn't defend me.

Still, he didn't protect me.

Still, he didn't acknowledge the storm he had created.

He slipped out of the car and into the house, leaving me alone with the woman he'd impregnated. She stared at me with a blankness that chilled my spirit. Then she went to her trunk.

I didn't register what was happening at first. Everything felt slow, disconnected, like my mind was struggling to catch up with the moment unfolding in front of me. It wasn't until she lifted the rusty car jack that reality snapped into focus.

Tiana stared at me with a look that made my stomach drop—hard, fixed, dangerous. For a split second, I was certain she was going to hit me with it. Then she spoke, her words slurred, sharp, and deliberate.

"Angela, Kai loves me. He's coming home with me and his child."

I told her, as calmly as I could, "Tiana, go home. Please."

The smell of liquor hit me then—strong, unmistakable. She was belligerent, unsteady, fueled by something deeper than anger. I could feel the situation slipping out of control, but my body hadn't caught up to the fear yet.

And then she swung.

The sound of shattering glass exploded through the air. It was loud, violent, finally. And in that instant, it felt like something inside me shattered too, whatever was left of denial, hope, or the illusion that this situation could still be contained.

That was the moment everything changed.

The sound of shattering glass felt like something breaking inside me.

She destroyed my windows while I stood there helpless, watching shards fall like rain. When she finally drove off, tires squealing, anger trailing behind her like smoke, I called the police with trembling hands.

He came back outside only after she was gone.

And somehow — somehow — I still let him come home with me.

The Second Attack

We stood by the window, the room lit only by the yellow glow of the parking lot lights. Below us, Tiana staggered toward my car, keys still in her hand, anger moving faster than logic.

"Oh my God," Kai said sharply. "She's really about to do this."

Metal scraped against metal. The sound sliced through me.

"That's my car," I whispered, my stomach dropping.

Kai stepped closer to the glass. "She's drunk. She's tripping. Nah — I'm about to go outside."

He turned toward the door, already moving.

"Kai," I said, louder now. "Stop."

"I'm not letting her tear up your car," he snapped. "I swear, I'm about to whoop her ass."

I moved between him and the door. "No. Don't touch her."

He looked at me like I'd lost my mind. "Angela, she's destroying your property."

"I know," I said, my voice shaking but steady. "And if you put your hands on her, this gets ten times worse."

"She deserves it," he said. "She's out of control."

"And she's drunk," I said firmly. "If you hit her and she falls or gets hurt, that's a whole different situation."

Another loud thud echoed from outside. I flinched.

"And look," I continued, pointing past him toward the car. "Her kids are in the back seat. Do you really want them watching their mother get hit?"

He froze.

"This is not something children should ever see," I said. "Not tonight. Not like this."

He ran his hand over his face, pacing. "So, we just let her do it?"

"We let the police handle it in the morning," I said. "We document everything. I have insurance. I can fix a car."

Another scrape. Another mark I couldn't yet see.

"But I can't fix what happens if you go out there," I added quietly.

He stopped pacing and looked back out the window. The anger in his shoulders slowly shifted into something heavier — helplessness, maybe.

"This is crazy," he muttered.

"Yes," I said. "It is. And chaos doesn't need another participant."

We stood there in silence, watching the destruction we couldn't stop without destroying something else in the process.

"Tomorrow," I said softly. "We'll handle it tomorrow."

He nodded, though his jaw was tight.

Outside, the damage continued.

Inside, I chose restraint — not because I was weak, but because someone had to be strong enough to end the scene without adding more trauma to it.

The morning after, I went outside to assess the damage, I stood in the parking lot longer than I meant to, staring at my car as it might explain itself if I waited long enough. The scratches ran deeper in the daylight. A dent along the side panel caught the sun in a way that felt almost cruel.

Kai came up beside me, hands on his hips.

"Damn," he said. "She really did a number on it."

I didn't answer right away. I traced the damage with my eyes instead.

"I didn't even want to look last night," I said quietly. "I knew if I did, I wouldn't sleep at all."

"She was drunk," he said. "She wasn't thinking."

I turned to him then. "She called me. Repeatedly. She threatened me."

He nodded, like he was processing facts instead of fear.

"Yeah. I figured."

Something in me tightened. "You figured?"

"She's emotional," he said. "That's how she gets."

I folded my arms, more to hold myself together than for warmth.

"This isn't just emotional," Kai. This is damaged. This is my property. This is my safety."

He exhaled slowly. "I know. I know. That's why we need to handle it the right way.".

He looked at the car again, then backed at me.

"We need go to the police station. File a report. Get it documented."

The word *police* landed heavier than I expected."

I nodded, though something in me wasn't settled.

"I don't want to do this out of anger," I said. "I'm tired of chaos."

"This isn't anger," he said. "This is just... handling it."

I looked back at my car, at the visible proof of a night I couldn't undo.

"It doesn't feel like handling it," I said softly. "It feels like cleaning up another mess I didn't make."

He didn't respond right away. Then, "We'll go together," he said. "I'll go with you."

Together. The word sounded reassuring, even as it rang hollow.

"Okay," I said finally. "Let's go."

Mercy

The officer looked me straight in the eyes and said, "Ma'am, you need to move. This isn't safe. It's only going to get worse." I nodded as if courage lived in me, though I felt none of it, carrying shame like a purse strapped to my side. When the District Attorney later called asking what I wanted to do with the case, anger whispered, *"Lock her up,"* but empathy countered, *"She's a mother... she's hurting too."* So, I chose mercy—probation, a restraining order, and restitution for the damage—because compassion had been stitched into my spirit long before trauma tried to unravel it. And after all of that, the betrayal, the violence, the danger, the humiliation, the financial loss, I still stayed with him. Because trauma can disguise itself as loyalty, and broken little girls sometimes choose familiar pain over unfamiliar healing. I hadn't yet learned that love is not proven through suffering, and I didn't know then that staying wasn't strength... it was survival masquerading as devotion.

CHAPTER SEVEN: When Hope Becomes a Trap

Opening Lesson: *Hope is holy until it asks you to stay where your soul is shrinking.*

There comes a moment in a woman's life when she looks in the mirror and no longer recognizes the eyes staring back. That's where I was — a stranger to myself, orbiting a man who treated me like an accessory to his chaos. I wasn't living; I was revolving, shrinking my entire world down to the circumference of his approval. And still, I stayed. Not because of love — real love nourishes. Not because of loyalty — loyalty requires truth. I stayed because I was chasing a promise that had never been real. I had crafted a holy-sounding illusion in my mind: *I will be his wife. I will be the first lady of his church. God will bless this once he changes. If I pray enough, cry enough, believe enough, it will all make sense.* Faith became something I gripped like a life raft even as it shredded in my hands. I told myself that "faith is the substance of things hoped for," and so I kept hoping for a man who belonged to someone else, for a covenant that didn't exist, for a blessing God never promised. Sometimes God does not rearrange the situation — sometimes He lets it unfold, lets the whispers grow louder, lets the warnings flash like neon signs, because He knows you won't leave until the pain becomes undeniable. And mine was on its way.

It arrived on an ordinary day when life slammed into me — literally. I had just finished a shift at my new job and was driving home in rush-hour traffic when a man struck the side of my car, sending my vehicle spinning across four lanes of interstate like a leaf caught in violent wind. Cars swerved, horns blared, and somehow — by the grace of God alone — nothing else collided with me.

My car came to rest in the grassy median, and for a moment I couldn't tell if I was alive or floating somewhere between worlds. A woman jumped out of her own car, breathless and shaken, shouting, *"Oh my God, are you okay? I almost hit you!"* Her voice felt distant, muffled by shock, as if I were watching the scene from somewhere outside my own body. But when I finally looked down and saw my ankle twisted in the wrong direction — bone visible, skin torn — reality snapped back hard and unforgiving.

The paramedics arrived fast.

"Ma'am, we don't know the internal damage," one of them said. "We have to use the jaws of life to cut you out of this car."

Metal groaned, doors bent, and then I was lifted into the air, helicopter blades chopping the sky above my broken body. And as I lay there in that helicopter, suspended between earth and heaven, a haunting truth settled over me:

I had been in a wreck long before that day —

a spiritual wreck,

an emotional wreck,

a psychological wreck —

and I had ignored every flashing hazard light.

The Man with a hidden agenda

News of the accident reached him quickly, and somewhere deep in my bruised, hopeful heart, a part of me still wanted him to show up like a knight in shining armor — to rush to my side, to choose me, to finally see my worth. But knights don't come wrapped in ulterior motives. He came, yes, but he came with an agenda. Anyone who understands lawsuits knows that money follows injuries, and the moment he sensed there might be a payout, his sudden "concern" became constant. He hovered. He called. He appeared. Not out of love, not out of compassion, but out of calculation. And when the settlement finally came through, it was substantial. I wish I could say I protected it, guarded it, held it close like the blessing it was. But pain makes generosity reckless, and loneliness makes your hands too open. Before I knew it, money was pouring out of me — to friends, to family, and yes... to him.

And when the money flowed, I saw a darkness in him that I had never allowed myself to see clearly. For years, I had witnessed his cruelty toward others, his manipulation, his deception, but he had never unleashed that side directly on me.

Until then, nothing changed.

No amount of money I spent stopped him from flaunting women in my face.

No love I gave softened his addictions or his hunger for attention.

No prayer I prayed transformed a man who had no intention of changing.

I prayed until my knees felt like cracked stone.

I begged God to fix him, reshape him, mold him into the man I believed he could be.

But the truth was simple and devastating:

He didn't want to change.

And God will not force a man to choose what he does not desire.

What I was fighting for wasn't transformation —

it was illusion.

The Beginning of the End

Some endings come with explosions.

Others arrive like the slow unraveling of a frayed rope.

This was both.

Little by little, the fog lifted.

Little by little, God peeled back the layers I had wrapped around him.

Little by little, I began to see him clearly:

The womanizer.

The manipulator.

The addict.

The man with a pulpit and a habit.

The man who preached deliverance but sowed destruction.

The man who quoted scripture but lived in contradiction.

The man I convinced myself God had assigned to me…

while he assigned himself to whoever fed his flesh that day.

I had spent so long trying to heal him

that I didn't realize I was the one bleeding out.

The accident broke my ankle.

But he had been breaking my spirit piece by piece.

And it was in those months — sitting with my leg elevated, trapped in stillness, wrapped in bandages and silence — that everything I had been running from finally caught up to me. I felt the weight of all I had lost, all I had given, all I had forgiven, and all I had ignored. The truth didn't arrive loudly; it settled into my spirit like a quiet revelation:

This was the beginning of the end.

CHAPTER EIGHT: The Shift that Saved Me

Opening Lesson: *One internal shift can reroute an entire destiny.*

There's a strange kind of quiet that comes after years of chaos. A quiet that feels like standing at the edge of yourself, unsure whether you're breaking apart or finally being rebuilt. That's where I was. A settlement check in my hand, a heart barely held together by prayers, and a soul exhausted from loving a man who had taken up far too much space in my life.

For the first time in a long time, I asked myself a question I had been too afraid to ask:

"What if my life could be different?"

I was tired — tired of call centers, tired of selling things for other people, tired of repeating the same cycle of bills, brokenness, survival, and emotional bruises. I didn't just want change.

I **needed** it.

Something in me — something buried under ten years of disappointment and spiritual exhaustion — was beginning to rise again.

And then the phone rang.

The Suggestion That Sparked My Life

It was my close friend, **Cherise** — the kind of woman who could hear your soul even when your voice trembled. I told her I had money now, but fear wrapped itself around my thoughts every time I considered spending it.

"What am I supposed to do with this?" I asked.

I don't want to be broke again. I can't go back.

Cherise chuckled softly, the kind of laugh that sounds casual but carries weight, and then she said it—half joking, half prophetic.

"Well... why don't you get your insurance license? You've been in sales forever. And hey," she added with a grin, "you don't have any felonies, so you're good to go."

We laughed. It felt light in the moment, almost throwaway humor. But somewhere beneath the laughter, something inside me shifted. I didn't dismiss it. I leaned in.

I listened as Cherise began sharing her story, how she'd built a career as a successful insurance agent, how the business had changed her life in ways she hadn't expected. She talked about stability. About growth. About opportunity. She spoke about how lucrative the industry had become, especially after the passing of new legislation, and how it opened doors for people willing to learn and commit.

As she talked, I felt it—that quiet stirring. Not excitement exactly, but recognition. Like a door I hadn't known existed was suddenly visible. What started as a joke lingered with me long after the conversation ended, settling into my thoughts, rearranging possibilities.

Sometimes purpose doesn't announce itself loudly.
Sometimes it slips into your life disguised as laughter—
and waits to see if you're paying attention.

"How do I do it?" I asked.

And just like that, a doorway opened —

not just to a career,

but to the woman I was becoming.

She gave me the steps — simple, straightforward, almost casual.

All I had to do was take a test.

And I had the one thing I'd never had before: time.

With the money from the lawsuit, I had taken an entire year off from work — something unheard of in my life. While he was out partying, drinking, chasing women and whatever else he could inhale or swallow, I was home with books in my lap and destiny tugging at my sleeve.

One-night, mid-study, I looked at Kai, this man who had eaten up a decade of my life and I said quietly, "This is going to change everything."

I didn't know then how true those words were.

The Match that Ignited Me

I wasn't the straight-A girl.

I wasn't the "gifted and talented" kid.

I wasn't the student teachers bragged about, or the one classmate whispered about in admiration.

In college, I was average—

hardworking, yes,

but unremarkable by the world's standards.

So, I never saw myself as particularly smart...

certainly not the kind of smart who passed state exams on the first try.

That felt like territory for people born with brilliance, not people who had to wrestle their way toward it.

But hunger?

Hunger will do what hope cannot.

And determination?

Determination will do what heartbreak never could.

I studied like a woman who had something to prove.

Not just to him—

though God knows he lit a fire he never meant to ignite.

But to myself.

To every version of me that ever doubted her worth.

To every younger me that settled

because she didn't know she could soar.

One evening, Cherise called me, her voice playful, teasing. She asked me about my progress while studying for the insurance exam. And then she dared me,

"Girl, I bet you won't pass that insurance exam on the first try," she laughed.

She meant nothing by it, just a joke, just a nudge.

But something in me snapped awake.

Something fierce.

Something fiery.

Something that had been buried under months of disappointment and spiritual exhaustion.

I looked at her through the phone as if she were in the room with me.

My voice went low, steady, almost dangerous.

"Oh, I bet you I will."

And I meant it.

I meant every syllable.

Because by then, I had collected enough fuel to power a resurrection.

Every disappointment from Kai

every lie he told...

every night he didn't come home...

every woman he dangled in my face like a weapon...

every prayer that felt unanswered...

every tear I swallowed to keep moving...

every wound I wrapped in silence...

I gathered it all.

Held it close.

And turned it into fire.

A holy fire.

A determined fire.

A fire that whispered:

"Watch me."

The Day Everything Changed

On the morning of my exam, Kai and I fell into one of those arguments that shake the walls — the kind where words become weapons and silence becomes a punishment you can feel in your bones. My heart was pounding, my spirit trembling, so I stepped outside to clear my head, hoping the air might calm the storm inside me.

When I came back, the house felt hollow.
Empty in a way I had never experienced before.

Everything I had ever bought him — the shoes, the socks, the underwear, the shirts — everything I had ever placed in his hands was gone.

Ten years of investment.

Ten years of tears.

Ten years of praying for a man who always, always chose himself.

And he chose to pull this stunt on the day of my exam —

the one day that had the power to change my future.

I was livid. Not just at him, but at myself for giving someone so broken that much access to my life.

But the truth is —

this didn't break me.

It awakened me.

It didn't destroy me; it sharpened me.

It didn't stop me; it pushed me forward.

And just like that, he walked out.

No goodbye.

No explanation.

No remorse — only empty hangers where his clothes used to be.

So, on that same day, with my heart bruised and my home stripped bare, I went to take my exam.

Before I left, I called my mother.

"Mom," I said, my voice cracking. *"Kai left."*

There was a brief pause on the other end of the line — just long enough for her to hear what my words were underneath. She knew that sound. It was the same one she carried when my father walked away from when I was 11 years old.

Then she spoke.

"What time is your exam?"

I blinked. *"What?"*

"What time are you scheduled to take the insurance exam, Angela?"

I swallowed. *"It's scheduled for 3:00 p.m."*

She paused again, this time longer. I could almost hear her checking the clock.

"Angela," she said slowly, *"it is 2:15."*

I sat there, gripping the phone, stunned.

Then her voice shifted to firm, commanding, and familiar.

"Get up and go take that exam."

I didn't move.

"Angela," she said again, louder now, *"GET UP."*

Still, I sat frozen.

And then she said it a third time — with authority that reached straight through my grief.

"Angela," I said

GET

UP

NOW!"

Something in me obeyed before my heart could argue.

And so, I did.

I walked into that testing center with chaos swirling in my head, heartbreak sitting heavy in my chest. But I pushed the noise aside and told myself:

If he could walk away that easily, then surely, I could walk into something new.

If he could leave me behind without hesitation, then I could choose myself without regret.

This test would be the doorway. My doorway.

So, I sat down.

I breathed.

I quit ten years of dysfunction.

And in that room, with everything in me trembling but determined…

I chose me.

The words didn't roar; they whispered.

But even in a whisper, they felt like a vow — a promise to the woman I had abandoned in the shadows of a man who never deserved her light.

If I pass this test, my life will never look like this again.

I said it under my breath, almost afraid to believe in the possibility of something better.

And then… I passed.

On the first try.

For a moment, I just stared at the screen, blinking through tears that didn't feel like sorrow anymore. The word **"PASSED"** glowed back at me, steady and sure, as if God Himself had typed it.

Something inside me cracked open —

but the breaking wasn't familiar this time.

It wasn't painful.

It wasn't heartbreak.

It wasn't disappointment slipping through my ribs.

It was **possibility**.

It was breath in a place that had felt suffocated.

It was light seeping into rooms I had kept locked.

It was the awakening of a woman who had been buried under ten years of chaos, confusion, and spiritual warfare.

I didn't just pass a test.

I crossed a threshold.

I stepped into a new chapter with trembling hands but a steady spirit.

And for the first time in a long time, I felt something rise in me that I had forgotten I possessed:

Hope.

Real hope.

Not the fragile hope I used to patch over his lies.

Not the desperate hope I used to justify staying.

But the kind of hope that stands tall, stretches wide, and whispers:

"Your life will never be the same again."

CHAPTER NINE: The Day the Spell Broke

Opening Lesson: *Deliverance begins the moment you choose clarity over attachment.*

Spiritual manipulation is a quiet thief.

It doesn't kick in the door.

It doesn't roar.

It doesn't arrive wearing horns or warning labels.

No

it slips in disguised as truth,

wrapped in Scripture,

delivered through the lips of someone who claims to love God

and claims to love you.

Webster describes it as "the use of religious or spiritual beliefs, teachings, or authority to control, influence, or exploit."

But definitions are clinical.

Cold.

Detached.

They don't capture the reality of what it feels like—

the way it twists your conscience,

the way it fogs your judgment,

the way it reshapes your understanding of right and wrong

until you cannot tell whether you're being led by God

or manipulated by someone who knows His language well enough to counterfeit it.

I didn't know I was being spiritually manipulated.

I didn't know that praying with someone could become a leash.

I didn't know that quoting Scripture could become a strategy.

I didn't know that "God told me..." could be a weapon—

one designed to bind a woman's heart

instead of healing it.

I didn't know because I loved God.

And I believed anyone who claimed to love Him the way I did

must be safe.

Must be genuine.

Must be aligned.

But predators do not always stalk in shadows.

Sometimes they walk in pulpits.

Sometimes they sit beside you during worship.

Sometimes they hold your hand while praying heaven down

and hell away.

The Image I Fell in Love With

Kai presented himself as Godly

God-fearing, spiritual, knowledgeable.

He prayed with authority.

He quoted Scripture fluently, effortlessly, like someone who breathed in Bible verses the way others breathed in air.

He spoke about spiritual warfare,
about blessings,
about destiny and calling,
with the tone of a man who had survived battles I could not imagine.

And I believed him.
I trusted him.
I aligned myself with him.

But what I fell in love with wasn't him—
*it was the **image** he carefully crafted.*

A projection.
A persona.
A performance designed to look holy
while hiding the hollowness underneath.

Kai wasn't building a relationship—
he was building a character.

The "godly man."
The "prayer warrior."
The "chosen one."
The "spirit-led partner."

I didn't fall in love with Kai.

I fell in love with the version of himself he created

to gain access to my spirit,

to my trust,

to my generosity,

to my purpose.

He preached the gospel.

He sang the gospel.

He prayed the gospel with a voice that could make a room stand still.

But he did not live it.

And no matter how holy the performance,

a tree is still known by the fruit it bears.

I didn't understand that then.

I was looking at the leaves —

the appearance of life, the show of growth, the illusion of spiritual depth.

But God does not judge by leaves.

He judges by fruit.

And the Fruits of the Spirit?

Love.

Joy.

Peace.

Patience.

Kindness.

Goodness.

Faithfulness.

Gentleness.

Self-control.

Not one of these grew from him.

Not love — because manipulation is not love.

Not joy — because joy doesn't need to drain someone else to feel alive.

Not peace — because his presence birthed confusion, not clarity.

Not patience — because impatience fueled the anger he hid behind charm.

Not kindness — because kindness doesn't cut you and call it care.

Not goodness — because goodness doesn't use people as stepping stones.

Not faithfulness — because faithfulness doesn't flirt with every open door.

Not gentleness — because gentleness doesn't turn harsh the moment it's challenged.

Not self-control — because self-control doesn't leave a trail of broken hearts and empty apologies.

He spoke Scripture,

but Scripture wasn't speaking through him.

He quoted verses,

but the verses never shaped his character.

He carried a Bible,

but the Bible did not carry him.

He knew how to sound Godly

without ever letting God transform him.

And that's when I learned:

A man can imitate the language of the Spirit

without ever possessing the Spirit Himself.

He can preach with fire,

pray with passion,

sing with conviction…

and still bear fruit that is rotten at the core.

I didn't fall in love with a godly man.

I fell in love with a godly image —

an imitation,

a costume,

a projection meant to charm women who loved the Lord.

But God is not mocked.

And eventually,

every tree reveals its fruit.

And the fruit he bore

was nothing like the Spirit he pretended to carry.

The More I Healed, the more the Illusion Cracked

It happened slowly at first — small realizations, little shifts, moments that didn't feel right.

But healing has a way of turning a dim lamp into a spotlight.

The more I stepped into my purpose,

the weaker his influence became.

The more I remembered who I was,

the more I could see who he really was.

The more I healed,

the more the illusion shattered.

And illusions always fight back when you stop believing in them.

Because once your eyes open...

once your spirit wakes up...

once God pulls the veil back...

A manipulator loses the only power he ever had —

the power of your blindness.

I wasn't blind anymore.

I wasn't desperate anymore.

And for the first time in a long time...

I wasn't afraid.

I could finally see the truth:

What I thought was love was a spiritual trap.

What I thought was connection was control.

What I thought was God was my hope dressed in his lies.

I wasn't rising because life was finally getting easier.

I was rising because God was trying to save me from him.

The Colorless Days

Depression swallowed me whole.

Food spoiled untouched.

Time blurred.

Colors faded.

The world went flat, lifeless, gray.

I wasn't just heartbroken.

I felt erased.

And that is what spiritual manipulation does

It convinces you that losing someone like him is a tragedy,

when in truth…

It is your deliverance.

But I didn't know that yet

He left me standing in the doorway of an apartment we shared

abandoned, depleted, confused, aching.

But the truth was:

His leaving wasn't my ending.

It was the beginning of my resurrection.

CHAPTER TEN: The Tactics: How Spiritual Manipulation Shows Up

Opening Lesson: *Naming the tactic is the first step toward breaking its power.*

Looking back over my story, I can now see every tactic he used — tactics I didn't have language for back then.

These signs, these warnings, these red flags — they were there all along:

1. Using God's Name to Justify Wrong Behavior

He knew how to pray with me.

He knew how to quote Scripture.

He knew how to talk about "calling," "purpose," and "God's will" — even while lying, cheating, and destroying my peace.

The Bible warns us of this:

"They come to you in sheep's clothing, but inwardly they are ravenous wolves."— Matthew 7:15

If someone can speak in tongues but cannot love with truth,

If someone can preach but cannot respect,

If someone can pray but cannot repent —They are not being led by the Holy Spirit, no matter what they say.

2. Studying Your Faith to Control You

He learned my devotion to God.

He studied how deeply I loved the Word.

He paid attention to my hunger for spiritual connection — and then he used it

When I questioned his behavior, he used Scripture as a shield:

"You're not being Christlike."

"You need to walk in forgiveness."

"A woman of God shouldn't question her man."

Those were not instructions — those were weapons.

The Bible calls this out plainly:

"For they bind heavy burdens, hard to bear… but they themselves will not move them with one finger."— Matthew 23:4

They demand what they don't live.

3. Confusing God's Voice with Their Own

He made me believe that disagreeing with him was disagreeing with God.

But Scripture says

"My sheep know MY voice, and a stranger they will not follow."— John 10:5

Any voice that drowns out your discernment,

any voice that silences your intuition,

any voice that shames you for asking questions is not God's voice.

4. Creating Emotional Dependency Through "Spiritual Intimacy"

Prayer became a leash.

Scripture became a rope.

Spiritual bonding became spiritual binding.

He knew that if he could connect to my soul spiritually, he could attach himself to my emotions and decisions. A man can pray with you and still not be sent by God.

The Warning Signs I Missed

When I reflect on my story with clarity, the signs were loud:

- I felt confused more than I felt peaceful.

- My self-worth decreased instead of increased.

- I feared disappointing him more than disappointing God.

- I ignored my convictions to keep the relationship alive.

- His "spirituality" felt performative, not transformative.

- My discernment grew quiet while his influence grew loud.

The Holy Spirit's voice brings clarity, peace, conviction, and guidance.

Manipulation brings confusion, chaos, and mental fog.

"God is not the author of confusion, but of peace."— 1 Corinthians 14:33

If peace is missing, God is not in it.

The Breaking of the Spell

When he left — that final day I found him packing everything I bought him and walking out of the door — I thought I was breaking.

In truth,

I woke up

Every spiritual chain snapped the moment his physical presence disappeared

And here is why:

Manipulation cannot survive distance.

It thrives on proximity, pressure, and repeated influence

Once I was alone once the noise left with him

I could finally hear God again.

How to Defeat Spiritual Manipulation

Deliverance isn't always a dramatic church moment.

Sometimes deliverance is clarity.

Sometimes deliverance is truth.

Sometimes deliverance is a man walking out so God can walk in.

Here is what sets a woman free:

1. Returning to God's Voice Over Man's Voice

I had to relearn the sound of God's whisper

I had to separate Scripture from control.

I had to pull my faith out of the hands of someone who misused it.

God's voice is gentle.

God's voice is loving and God's voice corrects but does not crush. Once I remembered that manipulation lost its power.

2. Regaining Your Identity

The moment I began studying for my insurance license…the moment I invested in my mind and my future…the moment I began bettering myself…his spiritual grip weakened.

Why? Because empowered women are hard to control. As I grew, he shrank. As I rose, he panicked. As I found purpose, he lost access.

3. Replacing Illusion with Truth

I had to face the truth that shook my spirit: I loved the idea of him more than the reality of him. The fantasy was godly.

The reality was demonic. Seeing truth is deliverance.

4. Accepting God's "No" as Protection

Sometimes God doesn't shut the door. He lets the person walk out.

Because if I had married him, If I had become his first lady,

If I had built a life with him…

It would not have fixed anything.

It would have destroyed me.

God's no was mercy.

God's no was protection.

God's no was the beginning of my yes.

The Empowerment: What I Know Now!

Spiritual manipulation loses its power when you:

- reclaim your identity

- reclaim your voice

- reclaim your purpose

- reclaim your discernment

- reclaim your relationship with God

I am living proof. When God set me free, He didn't just rescue me from a man

He rescued me from the version of myself that believed manipulation was love.

What I endured became the soil of the woman I am now, stronger, wiser, bolder, and spiritually clear. And in the story of my life, that chapter of spiritual manipulation will never be my identity...

but it will always be my testimony.

CHAPTER ELEVEN: THE RISING — When God Restores What Was Stolen

Opening Lesson: *Restoration isn't returning to who you were; it's becoming who you were always meant to be.*

Healing is not a moment.

It is a return. Returning to yourself, to your purpose, to the parts of you that were buried in pain and spiritual fog.

After leaving, I had to climb out of the emotional wreckage he left behind. Depression had swallowed my world so deeply that I forgot what color looked like. My joy was strange. My confidence was a memory.

But God specializes in resurrections.

What the enemy thought would destroy me became the very place where God rebuilt me.

The Rebuilding of Me

When the manipulation ended, I didn't just get free. I got empty.

Empty enough for God to refill me.

Empty enough for purpose to take root.

Empty enough to step into the destiny that had been waiting for me all along.

Working in the insurance industry had already awakened me. It gave me stability. It gave me confidence. It reintroduced me to my worth. I started to see that I had a mind, a sharp, capable, powerful mind — that had been dormant under years of distraction and emotional captivity.

But healing didn't stop there.

A hunger rose in me.

A hunger to grow.

A hunger to learn.

A hunger to reclaim what I had given up.

And that hunger led me right back to school.

Higher Education

The day I decided to go back to college, it felt like stepping into a version of myself I had abandoned years earlier. Tuition forms, textbooks, online classes — it all looked so ordinary on the outside. But inside, something sacred was stirring. I could feel God gently nudging me forward, whispering possibility into places that had once held only fear.

I remember asking Him, almost trembling:

"Why now? Why send me back after all these years?" Lord 10 years have passed by so quickly but why now?

And God responded — not with thunder, not with force, but with a whisper as clear as sunlight warming a windowpane:

"The first time, I wasn't in it.
But this time… I am."

And when God is in something, *nothing* can stop it.

Not fear.

Not self-doubt.

Not age.

Not time.

Not the lies I once believed about myself.

Not the wounds I thought were too deep to heal.

Because when God breathes on a thing it rises.

Discovering the Woman I had Forgotten

College became so much more than education, it became **deliverance**.

I discovered that I wasn't just smart, **I was exceptional.**

I wasn't just capable, **I was brilliant.**

And I wasn't simply surviving anymore, **I was rising.**

While working full-time in the insurance industry...

While healing from heartbreak...

While recovering from manipulation and spiritual deception...

While rebuilding my voice, my confidence, my life...

I maintained a **4.0 GPA**.

I graduated in the **top 5%** of my class.

I earned my degree in **Healthcare Administration** — and I earned it with honor, excellence, and a newfound reverence for the woman God created me to be.

I walked into classrooms burdened with fear...

and walked out covered in honor.

I began assignments questioning my worth...

and finished them writing papers that stunned professors.

I entered the program as a woman once broken...

and I graduated as a woman **restored**.

Every A was a brick laid in the rebuilding of my confidence.

Every lecture mastered was a piece of my identity returned.

Every demonstration of excellence was God whispering:

"You were always this. You just forgot."

What the Enemy Stole, God Returned

Scripture promises us:

"I will restore to you the years that the locust has eaten." — *Joel 2:25*

And when I walked across that graduation stage, I didn't just receive a degree

I received **restoration**, **validation**, and **vindication**.

What manipulation stole from me,

God restored to me.

What heartbreak buried,

God resurrected.

What trauma silenced,

God amplified into purpose.

I didn't just heal —**I returned.**

To myself.

To my mind.

To my calling.

To the woman I was always meant to be.

The Woman I Became

Returning to school taught me something profound:

I am far more intelligent than I ever believed.

Far more beautiful than I ever saw.

Far more powerful than I ever realized.

Healing doesn't just mend wounds —

it reveals identity.

Rebuilding doesn't just restore what was lost —

it introduces you to the woman you were born to be.

In the ashes of abandonment,

God built a scholar.

In the ruins of manipulation,

God built a leader.

In the aftermath of betrayal,

God built a woman with vision, purpose, and strength.

My degree wasn't just an accomplishment —

it was a **divine declaration**:

You survived.

You rose.

You reclaimed everything that was taken.

And this time —

this new chapter,

this new identity,

this new purpose —

God was in it from the very first step.

Epilogue

Posture Shift: *I Survived the Man That I Prayed For*

There comes a moment in every woman's life when she realizes that the position she held onto for far too long was never the posture God intended for her to stay in. Healing taught me that. Pain taught me that. And God whispered it through every closed door, every unraveling illusion, every quiet night where I thought the story was over.

A posture shift is not a small adjustment.

It is a spiritual realignment —

a turning of the soul,

a divine recalibration.

For years, I bent myself toward a man who did not honor me.

I curved my worth around his wounds.

I folded myself inward trying to hold together a relationship that God never authored.

But God allowed what I thought would break me... to reposition me.

The heartbreak wasn't the ending.

The manipulation wasn't the curse.

The depression wasn't the final sentence.

They were all part of the shift.

Because what I didn't know then — what I couldn't yet see — was that God was preparing me to rise into a new posture, a new identity, and a new strength.

And today, I stand firmly in this truth:

I survived the man that I prayed for.

That sentence alone carries the weight of my testimony.

I prayed with sincerity.

I loved with loyalty.

I held onto the fantasy longer than I held onto the reality.

But when God pried my fingers away,

when He removed what I thought I needed,

when He exposed what was never meant to go with me...

He didn't abandon me.

He *rescued* me.

When he walked out, I thought I was losing everything.

But God was removing the weight that kept me bent.

When I cried and wondered why God didn't change him,

God was quietly changing *me*.

When I begged God to fix what was breaking,

He was preparing me to break free.

Because God never turned His back on me.

I never fell out of love with God — in fact, it was God's love that carried me through every dark moment of this story. Through every heartbreak, every confusion, every deception, I clung to Him. My faith never failed. My Christianity did not shatter. I did not curse God. I did not walk away from the church.

If anything, this journey deepened my reverence for Him.

I learned that God is not the author of abuse.

God does not send confusion.

God does not wrap manipulation in Scripture.

People misuse faith — God never does.

I am not angry with God.

I am not angry at the church.

And I do not hate men.

This book is not a weapon against the male gender.

It is not an attack.

It is not bitterness wrapped in spirituality.

This is simply **my story** —

my experience,

my survival,

my testimony.

And my purpose is pure:

To help women and men recognize spiritual manipulation

To expose the tricks and strategies of the enemy

To prevent someone else from mistaking a snare for a blessing

To guide others toward healing, clarity, and discernment

Because the devil studies the faithful.

He targets the sincere.

He manipulates through familiarity, comfort, and even religion.

If my story enlightens even one soul,

saves even one heart,

wakes up even one spirit—

Then none of my suffering was wasted.

A posture shift isn't about where your body stands.

It's about where your spirit settles.

And now...

my spirit stands tall.

My voice stands strong.

My heart stands whole.

My purpose stands rooted.

My identity stands restored.

I once prayed for a man who was never mine.

Now I pray for the woman I am becoming —

and I love her too much to ever bend the wrong way again.

The enemy tried to bend me.

Manipulation tried to silence me.

Heartbreak tried to bury me.

But God corrected my posture.

And as I step into the fullness of who I am —

unapologetic, restored, wise, and spiritually aligned —

I declare:

I survived the man that I prayed for...

and the woman I became is my victory.

This is my epilogue.

And also my beginning.

My shift.

My rise.

My alignment.

My Posture Shift.

A Blessing for the Reader

God of truth and tenderness, I lift every reader holding these pages — woman or man, weary or hopeful, certain or still searching. You see the places they have not named aloud, the questions they carry quietly, the moments they stayed longer than they should have because love, faith, or fear told them to endure.

If this story stirred memories they tried to bury, meet them with gentleness.
If it brought clarity that feels both freeing and painful, steady their heart as truth settles in.

For the reader who has been confused, restore discernment without shame.
For the reader who has been manipulated, return their trust — first in You, and then in themselves. For the reader who has caused harm,
 grant humility, accountability, and the courage to choose healing over control.

Teach us all the difference between devotion and self-abandonment, between spiritual intimacy and spiritual authority, between love that nurtures and love that consumes.

May no one leave these pages feeling condemned or small. Instead, let them leave feeling seen, strengthened, and whole. Remind them that clarity is not cruelty, boundaries are not betrayal, and walking away can be an act of faith.

And for the one still standing at the crossroads —give peace where there is turmoil, wisdom where there is noise, and the courage to choose life, truth, and freedom.

Amen.

Dear Heavenly Father

I come to You with a grateful heart. Thank You for the posture shift — for the transformation I could not have orchestrated on my own. Thank you for keeping Your hand on me during a time when I was uncertain, when my vision was clouded, and I could not clearly see the way forward.

You guided me when clarity felt distant. You protected me when I didn't yet know what to ask for. You held me steady when my faith was being tested. Even in moments of confusion, you were present — working, covering, and leading me toward truth.

I am grateful for all that You have done in my life — the seen and the unseen, the answered prayers and the lessons that came wrapped in waiting. This journey, this growth, and this healing are my testimonies.

I now understand that *all things work together for the good of those who are called according to the Lord's purpose.*

This story, this becoming, this restoration — it was orchestrated by you.

Amen.

Made in the USA
Coppell, TX
24 February 2026

72253924R00079